Animals After Dark

RACCOONS

SCAVENGERS OF THE NIGHT

Elaine Landau

WORDS TO KNOW

adapt—To survive in a new place.

Algonquin—An American Indian group.

den—The home of an animal.

hibernate—To sleep deeply through the winter.

nocturnal—Active at night.

predator—An animal that hunts other animals for food.

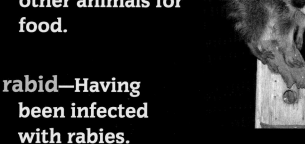

rabid—Having been infected with rabies.

rabies—A disease that attacks the brain and spinal cord.

CONTENTS

Raccoons sometimes raid garbage cans at night.

4

A RAIDER IN THE NIGHT

You are camping with your family on a hot summer night. Everyone has gone to sleep. Suddenly, there is a loud crash. It wakes up everyone. Has someone or something tipped over the garbage can near the tent?

You and your parents rush out to see. Sure enough, a furry animal is going through the trash. The creature looks up at you. Your nighttime raider is a raccoon.

INTRODUCING THE RACCOON

Most people know a raccoon when they see one. These creatures are hard to mistake for other animals. They have short oval ears, a pointed snout, and a black nose. But they are best known for the black mask around their eyes. Raccoons also have brown fur rings around their tails.

These animals are between two and three feet long. That includes their ten-inch bushy tail. Males are usually larger than females. Raccoons in the north tend to be larger than southern raccoons, too.

A raccoon looks like it has a mask around its eyes.

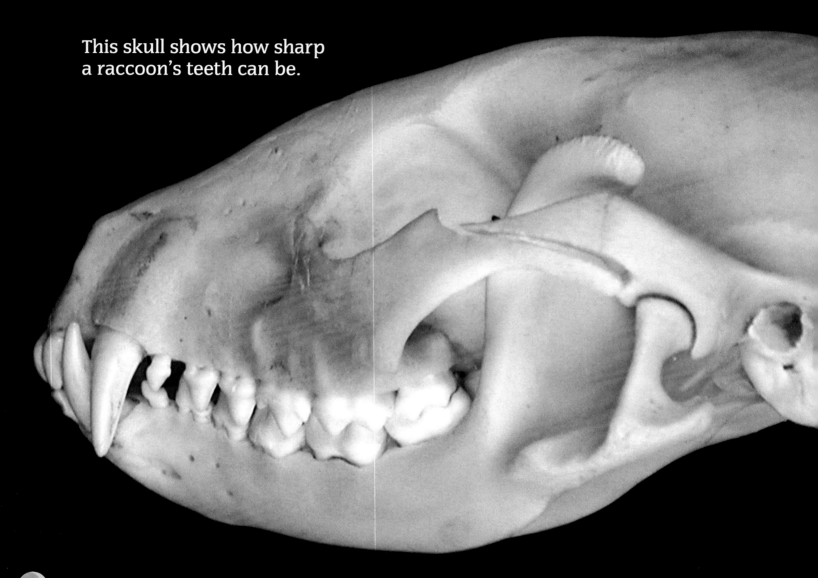

This skull shows how sharp a raccoon's teeth can be.

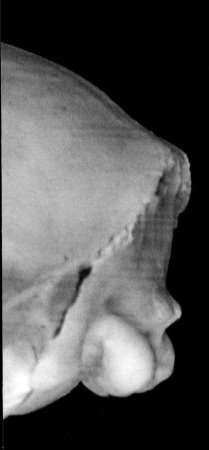

Raccoons vary in color. They usually have long, thick grayish fur. However, raccoons in some parts of the United States have reddish-brown fur. A raccoon's belly is light colored.

A raccoon's front paws look like thin human hands. Each paw has five fingers. Raccoons can do a lot of things with their fingers. They can easily turn a doorknob or open a refrigerator door. Raccoons have even turned on water faucets!

The raccoon's name comes from the Algonquin (al-gon-kwen) Indian word *aroughcoune*. It means "he scratches with his hand." The name describes the raccoon's fingers well.

ALL ABOUT RACCOONS

When Christopher Columbus first saw a raccoon, he called it a "clown-like dog." Today, we know that both raccoons and dogs belong to a group of animals called carnivores. Carnivores are animals that like to eat meat.

Raccoons are strong for their size. They are also very athletic. They can quickly climb up or down a tree. They are also good swimmers and runners. Raccoons can run as fast as fifteen miles per hour.

Raccoons are very good at climbing trees. This raccoon is climbing a tree in California.

Raccoons may look cute but will fight fiercely if cornered. If attacked by a dog, they will rip at its body with their teeth and claws. Raccoons have killed dogs.

Raccoons live in Canada, the United States, and in Mexico and parts of Central America. In very cold areas, raccoons are not active during the winter. They remain in their dens, or homes. However, they are not truly hibernating, or sleeping deeply through the winter.

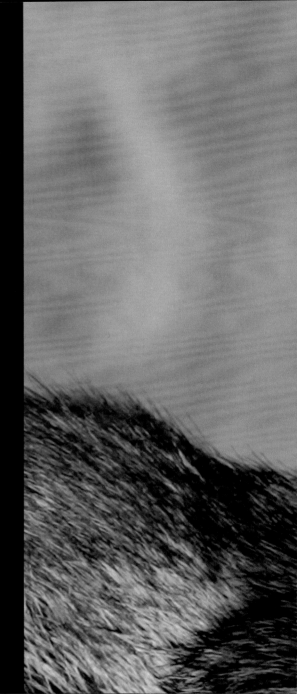

Raccoons can be very fierce.

Raccoons can easily see
a person in the dark.

NIGHT LIFE

    Raccoons are nocturnal. They rest during the day and are active at night. Their bodies are good for night life. Raccoons hear well. This helps them find prey after dark. It is also useful in avoiding predators. They can hear an enemy come near them.

    Raccoons also see very well in the dark. Since raccoons come out at night, they are not often seen. At times, people may not even know that raccoons are living nearby.

HUNTING AND EATING

Though they are called carnivores, raccoons are really omnivores when it comes to their meals. This means they will eat both animals and plants. They eat turtle eggs, bird eggs, berries, nuts, and insects. They have also been known to grab food from bird feeders, farmers' fields, and garbage bags.

Raccoons really enjoy crayfish, frogs, clams, and mussels they find in shallow waters. Raccoons feel for their prey in the water with their front paws.

Wherever they get their food, raccoons dunk it in water before eating it.

The raccoon's scientific name is *Procyon lotor (Pro-see-on low-tore)*. "Lotor" means "the washer." It may look like raccoons are washing their food. But, it is more likely that they are just carefully feeling their food. This is done to make sure there are no sharp bones or dangerous pieces in it.

This raccoon dips food in a stream in Oklahoma.

A hole in a tree can
be a very safe place
for a raccoon.

WHERE THE RACCOONS ARE

Raccoons are often found in the woods near water. They also live in marshes, fields, and even in cities.

Raccoons' homes include hollow trees as well as burrows, or holes in the ground, left by other animals. Raccoons also live in brush piles, haystacks, caves, mines, or empty buildings.

In towns and cities, these wild animals often live very close to humans. They may be found in chimneys, sewers, under decks, or in people's attics. They often look for food in garbage cans. They tip over the cans and search for a tasty surprise inside.

PREDATORS

Raccoons in the wild have enemies. Coyotes, bobcats, and wolves eat them. Large owls, foxes, and badgers go after raccoon babies. Their mothers try to protect them, but sometimes raccoon babies are killed.

Raccoons die in other ways as well. They are often run over by cars and trucks or killed by human hunters. Some also die from disease.

Raccoons can live up to ten years in the wild. However, most only live for about two to three years.

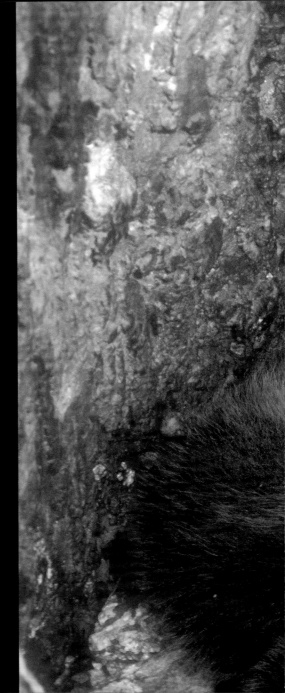

These raccoon babies sleep safely away from predators.

21

RAISING YOUNG

Raccoon babies do not know how to climb trees at first. Their mothers have to teach them.

Raccoons usually live alone. Yet they come together to mate from January to March. A female raccoon is ready to mate when she is a year old. Males begin to mate when they are two years old. About two months after mating, females give birth to babies.

Usually from four to six babies are born. These young raccoons are helpless. They are born without teeth and with their eyes shut. Raccoon babies have hardly any fur. They depend on their mother for everything.

The young raccoons can stand when they are a little more than a month old. But their mother does not take them out of the den until they are three or four months old. She will teach them to hunt and climb trees. They stay with their mother for about the first year of their lives. After that, they are on their own.

RACCOONS AND PEOPLE

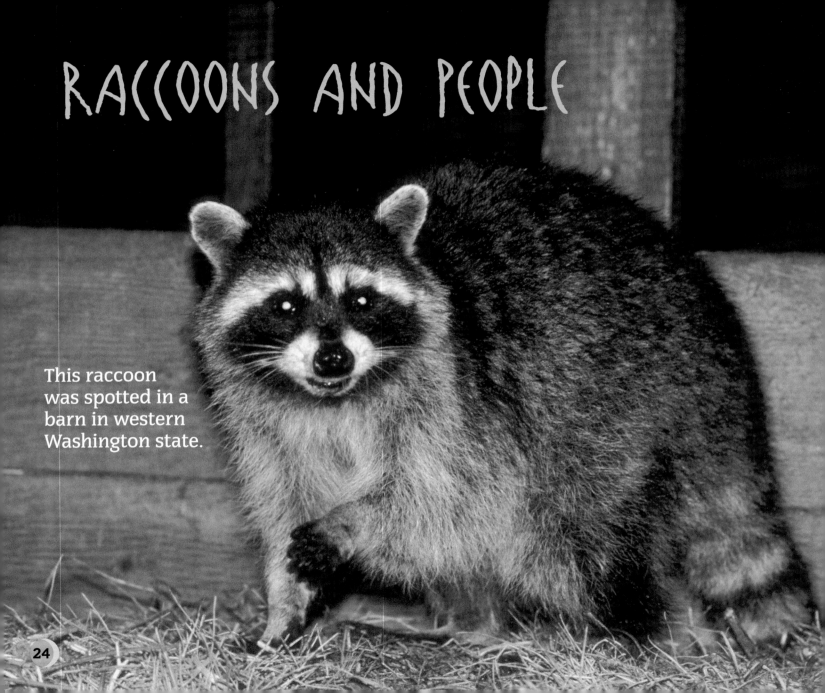

This raccoon was spotted in a barn in western Washington state.

Humans have hunted and trapped raccoons since early times. In North America, people in the 1700s ate raccoon meat. They used the raccoon skins to make clothing. Many of them wore "coonskin" caps.

In the 1920s, raccoon fur coats were in fashion. Women also wore fancy raccoon hats.

Today, fewer people wear furs. Also, fewer people eat raccoons. However, some people still hunt them.

Other people view raccoons as pests. These animals eat fruit and vegetables from people's gardens. Raccoons sometimes build dens near people's homes as well.

Still other people have raccoons as pets. However, this is not a good idea. In many states, it is against the law to own a raccoon.

A wild raccoon that walks up to you or does not run away may actually be ill. Raccoons can carry diseases like rabies. A human can get rabies and die if bitten or scratched by a rabid raccoon. So, it is best to enjoy raccoons from a distance.

THE FUTURE

There are more raccoons every year. Less and less people are killing them. Raccoons also adapt well to their surroundings. They will eat just about anything and build dens just about anywhere.

Over the years, humans have cut down trees and built homes. Once raccoons have fewer forests to live in, they start to come to people's yards more often. As this continues, we are likely to see still more raccoons around us.

These creatures have their place in the world. So do people. Both can easily live near one another if people respect wildlife.

Sometimes, raccoons look for seeds in a birdhouse. Other times, they try to eat bird eggs or babies.

FUN FACTS ABOUT RACCOONS

* Raccoons are at least as smart as dogs and cats.

* Because raccoons are night animals, few people hear the sounds they make. But raccoons hiss, whistle, scream, and growl.

* A raccoon can easily lift a dime out of a shirt pocket with its fingers.

* The heaviest raccoon weighed sixty-two pounds.

* The oldest raccoon lived for twenty-one years.

Raccoons are very good at jumping.

BOOKS

Crossingham, John, and Bobbie Kalman. *The Life Cycle of a Raccoon.* New York: Crabtree, 2003.

Jacobs, Lee. *Raccoon.* San Diego, Calif.: Blackbirch Press, 2002.

Kite, Patricia. *Raccoons.* Minneapolis, Minn.: Lerner, 2004.

Ripple, William John. *Raccoons.* Minneapolis, Minn.: Pebble Books, 2006.

INTERNET ADDRESSES

PAWS—Kids Who Care

This Web site has lots of great facts about raccoons.

<http://www.pawskids.org/ >

Click on "Wildlife" at the left. Select "Wildlife Gallery." Click on "Raccoon."

Raccoon Rescue

Read about people that rescue raccoons and move them to safe places.

<http://www.raccoonrescue. com>

Enslow Elementary, an imprint of Enslow Publishers, Inc.

Enslow Elementary® is a registered trademark of Enslow Publishers, Inc.

Library of Congress Cataloging-in-Publication Data

Landau, Elaine.
    Raccoons : scavengers of the night / Elaine Landau.
      p. cm. — (Animals after dark)
    Includes bibliographical references and index.
    ISBN-13: 978-0-7660-2767-1
    ISBN-10: 0-7660-2767-8
    1. Raccoons—Juvenile literature. I. Title. II. Series.
  QL737.C26L36 2006
  599.76′32—dc22   2006014968

Printed in the United States of America

10 9 8 7 6 5 4 3 2

To Our Readers: We have done our best to make sure all Internet Addresses in this book were active and appropriate when we went to press. However, the author and the publisher have no control over and assume no liability for the material available on those Internet sites or on other Web sites they may link to. Any comments or suggestions can be sent by e-mail to comments@enslow.com or to the address on the back cover.

Series Literacy Advisor: Dr. Allan A. De Fina, Department of Literacy Education, New Jersey City University.

Illustration Credits: © Aistov Alexey, Shutterstock.com, pp. 12–13; © ANDERSON, VICKI/Animals Animals–Earth Sciences–All rights reserved., pp. 24–25; © Bill Frische, Shutterstock.com, pp. 2 (right), 27; © DEGGINGER, E.R./Animals Animals–Earth Sciences–All rights reserved., pp. 20–21; © Gloria H. Chomica/Masterfile, pp. 6–7; © Joe McDonald/Visuals Unlimited, pp. 28–29; Mack Reed, © 2006 iStock International, Inc., pp. 8–9; © Micha Fleuren, Shutterstock.com, pp. 2 (bottom left), 32; © Michael Durham/Visuals Unlimited, pp. 4–5; Phil A. Dotson/Photo Researchers, Inc., pp. 16–17; © Richard C. Bennett, Shutterstock.com, pp. 14–15, 28 (bottom left); © Rob and Ann Simpson/Visuals Unlimited, pp. 18–19; © Scott Rothstein, Shutterstock.com, p. 3; Shutterstock.com, p. 1; © Steve Maslowski/Visuals Unlimited, pp. 22–23; U.S. Fish and Wildlife Service, pp. 2 (top left), 10–11.

Cover Illustration: Shutterstock.com

Enslow Elementary
an imprint of

 Enslow Publishers, Inc.
40 Industrial Road
Box 398
Berkeley Heights, NJ 07922
USA

http://www.enslow.com